Samuel French Acting Edition

Ethan Frome

by Gary L. Blackwood

Adapted from the Novel by
Edith Wharton

Copyright © 2001 by Gary L. Blackwood
All Rights Reserved

ETHAN FROME is fully protected under the copyright laws of the United States of America, the British Commonwealth, including Canada, and all other countries of the Copyright Union. All rights, including professional and amateur stage productions, recitation, lecturing, public reading, motion picture, radio broadcasting, television and the rights of translation into foreign languages are strictly reserved.

ISBN 978-0-874-40139-4

www.SamuelFrench.com
www.SamuelFrench.co.uk

For Production Enquiries

United States and Canada
Info@SamuelFrench.com
1-866-598-8449

United Kingdom and Europe
Plays@SamuelFrench.co.uk
020-7255-4302

Each title is subject to availability from Samuel French, depending upon country of performance. Please be aware that *ETHAN FROME* may not be licensed by Samuel French in your territory. Professional and amateur producers should contact the nearest Samuel French office or licensing partner to verify availability.

CAUTION: Professional and amateur producers are hereby warned that *ETHAN FROME* is subject to a licensing fee. Publication of this play(s) does not imply availability for performance. Both amateurs and professionals considering a production are strongly advised to apply to Samuel French before starting rehearsals, advertising, or booking a theatre. A licensing fee must be paid whether the title(s) is presented for charity or gain and whether or not admission is charged. Professional/Stock licensing fees are quoted upon application to Samuel French.

No one shall make any changes in this title(s) for the purpose of production. No part of this book may be reproduced, stored in a retrieval system, or transmitted in any form, by any means, now known or yet to be invented, including mechanical, electronic, photocopying, recording, videotaping, or otherwise, without the prior written permission of the publisher. No one shall upload this title(s), or part of this title(s), to any social media websites.

For all enquiries regarding motion picture, television, and other media rights, please contact Samuel French.

Please refer to page 62 for further copyright information.

CHARACTERS

Men:

ETHAN FROME, 30's
EDWARD, 20's
ANDREW HALE, 50's-60's
DENIS EADY, 20's
NED, 20's

Women:

MATTIE SILVER, 20's
ZEENA FROME, 30's-40's
MRS. HALE, 50's-60's
RUTH, 20's

PLAYING TIME

90-100 minutes without intermission

SET

A single, simple set with various playing areas

ETHAN FROME

a stage play adapted from the novel by Edith Wharton

(Various areas of the stage represent parts of the town of Starkfield, MA. At Stage Left is an area that serves as the Frome farmhouse. It consists of a dining table with three chairs, a wood cookstove, a set of cupboards with a sink, and a short flight of stairs that leads offstage Left. Downstage of this are a couple of gravestones that represent the family cemetery.)

(Right of Center is a buckboard wagon, minus the horses. The Right half of the buckboard seat is designed to swivel, so that the person sitting in it can face away from the audience. An alternative is a platform with a buckboard seat. Upstage and to the Right of this is a single chair that represents the interior of Eady's General Store.)

(The play takes place in two different time periods. One is Winter, and the lighting is appropriately wintry. In this time period, ETHAN FROME is a middle-aged man whose face and body are twisted from an accident. No special makeup is used to convey this, just the way the actor carries himself. Ethan also wears a heavy coat during the Winter parts. In the Summer period, the lighting is brighter and more summery. Ethan is dressed in shirtsleeves and

carries himself normally, like a man of about thirty.)

(At Lights Up, EDWARD, a city fellow in his early twenties, carrying a valise, and dressed in turn of the century clothing, crosses to Stage Right, where ANDREW HALE, a stout man in his fifties or sixties, stands.)

EDWARD. Good afternoon.
HALE. Passable.
EDWARD. Is this the livery stable?
HALE. That's what the sign says.
EDWARD. I was wondering about the possibility of renting some sort of rig, and possibly a driver, to take me out to Corbury Junction.
HALE. Corbury Junction, eh? Something to do with that new power house they're building out that way, I expect?
EDWARD. Yes, as a matter of fact. I'm checking up on the progress of it.
HALE. You must be one of them engineers, then.
EDWARD. That's right.
HALE. They pay you right smart for that, do they?
EDWARD. I do well enough, yes. Well. What are the chances of getting a rig of some sort?
HALE. Not so good just now. Piss poor, in fact, you might say. Every head I've got has come down with the strangles.
EDWARD. Oh. I'm very sorry to hear that.
HALE. So'm I; so'm I. Best bet I know of would be to catch a ride with somebody going out that way.

EDWARD. But I - I'd be wanting to come back again this evening.

HALE. That is a problem. *(nods at the wagon)* You see that wagon there, with the bays hitched to it? Belongs to a fella named Ethan Frome. He lives out toward Corbury Junction. I believe he'd be glad enough to drive you the extra distance.

EDWARD. But I don't even know the man. Why would he go out of his way for me?

HALE. I don't know as he would. But I know he wouldn't be sorry to earn a dollar. Help him pay for all that patent medicine he buys.

EDWARD. Oh? Is he ill?

HALE. Not exactly. The medicine's for his wife. She takes it like candy. I doubt there's any medicine made that'll cure what ails him.

EDWARD. What do you mean?

HALE. See for yourself.

(ETHAN ENTERS at Up Left with a sack of feed and crosses to the wagon. He is as stiff and stooped as an octagenarian. His limp is so pronounced he seems in constant danger of falling. His mouth is skewed, and one eye squints. Despite all that, he's obviously a powerful man)

HALE *(cont)*. He's been that way ever since the smash-up.

EDWARD. Smash-up? It must have been a serious one.

HALE. Enough to kill most men. But the Fromes are tough stock. He'll most likely live to be hundred.

EDWARD. A hundred? Good God. He looks as if he were dead and in Hell now.

(Ethan goes off, returns with several library books, puts them under the buckboard seat)

HALE. Guess he's been in Starkfield too many winters. Most of the smart ones get away.

EDWARD. Why didn't he?

HALE. Somebody had to stay and care for the folks. There wasn't ever anybody but Ethan. First his father, then his mother, then his wife. And then the smash-up. He had to stay then.

EDWARD. Well. I thank you for your help. I hope your horses are back on their feet soon.

HALE. And I hope that power house of yours don't blow itself up.

EDWARD. It won't. *(approaches Ethan)* Mr. Frome? The man at the livery stable mentioned that you might be willing to provide me with transportation to Corbury Junction. I'd be happy to pay you, of course.

ETHAN. I don't mind. *(climbs onto the seat)* I guess you'd better get in.

EDWARD. Oh. Right.

(He puts his valise in and climbs up. Ethan flicks the reins and clucks his tongue. The two men rock slightly to simulate the motion of the wagon.)

EDWARD *(cont, uncomfortable)*. As you've probably guessed, I'm on my way out there to check on the progress of the power plant. I inspect plants all over the country. *(no reply)* I gathered that the fellow at the livery was a bit skeptical about the prospect of widespread electrification. I was wondering if that represents the prevailing attitude around this part of the state. Mr. Frome?

> *(They stop rocking. Ethan stares Down Center, where the figure of MATTIE SILVER appears in low light. She is about twenty, frail and pretty, but lively. She has a traveling trunk.)*

EDWARD *(cont)*. Mr. Frome? *(looks up and down a set of imaginary tracks)* There's no train coming. I don't think we need to - Mr. Frome? Is anything wrong?
ETHAN. No. Just . . . recalling.

> *(As he goes on staring, the lights go down on him and come up on Mattie. Edward swivels in his seat, away from the audience. Ethan sheds his coat and his twisted stance and climbs down into the light.)*

MATTIE. Cousin Ethan?
ETHAN. I guess you must be Miss Silver.
MATTIE. Mattie. Call me Mattie, please.
ETHAN. Let me help you with that trunk.

(He swings it effortlessly into the wagon bed)

MATTIE. Thank you. I - I thought Cousin Zeena would be with you.
ETHAN. She would have, but she's been feeling more poorly than usual. *(He sees that she is waiting to be helped*

into the wagon.) Oh. Sorry. I'm not used to - *(Helps her in. To horses)* Go 'long.

MATTIE. I'm sorry to hear that Zeena's under the weather. She never does feel very well, does she? It must be a trial for you, having to keep up the farm and the mill, and do for Zeena on top of it all.

ETHAN *(shrugs).* A person does what's wanted.

MATTIE. Of course. *(brightly)* Anyway, that's what I'm here for, isn't it? To take some of the burden off you and Zeena. I may not look like much of a one for work, but I'll earn my keep, I promise you. I believe I'd as soon do most anything as to stand behind a department store counter like I've been doing. Not that the work itself was so bad. It was just having to stand in one place all day. It's murder on your feet. I ain't complaining, mind you. I was happy enough to have the work. And then there were the customers - the *clientele*, they insisted on us calling them. *(laughs)* Do you know, I once had a lady bring back a bottle of perfume with only this much in the bottom, and ask to exchange it? Said she never could get fond of the scent. *(laughs again. Ethan doesn't respond. In fact, he looks a little annoyed)* "It smells like pennyroyal," she said. I almost said to her, in that case she ought to use it for insect spray. But of course I didn't. It's too bad, isn't it, that a person can't just go ahead and do what they feel like sometimes? Still and all, working in the city did have its good points. Oh, I'm not saying I mind coming here. I'm sure I'll like it here just fine, too. It's just that there's always something to do in the city-dances, theatre, recitals. Didn't you ever think you might care to live in the city? Ethan?

ETHAN *(she's struck a nerve).* I've thought about it, yes.

(a silence)

MATTIE. You don't approve of me coming here. Do you?

ETHAN. I never said that.

MATTIE. You didn't have to. I can see it in your face. Well, I guess I can't blame you. First your mama's illness, and now Zeena's troubles. I guess the last thing you need is another woman around that's more hindrance than help. Well, let me tell you, I mean to do my best to keep up my end of the bargain. I ain't strong, and I never had anybody to show me about keeping house and such, but I learn fast, and I'm willing, and I'll see to it that you're not sorry you took me in.

ETHAN. I'm not sorry.

MATTIE. You're not happy, either.

ETHAN. That's nothing to do with you. *(pause)* I suppose I'm just not used to so much talk.

MATTIE. I'm sorry. I do go on sometimes, I know. I guess it's because I'm nervous.

ETHAN. It's all right. It's like I said, I just ain't used to it. At least you ain't a fretter. So much of what passes for conversation in Starkfield is just some form of complaining.

MATTIE. No, I ain't the sort to complain much. *(Trying to be cheerful)* It's awful beautiful up here, ain't it? It looks just like a painted landscape.

ETHAN. You like art, do you?

MATTIE. Oh, yes. On my days off, I used to spend hours at the museum, looking at the paintings. I never did get to spend much time out in the country, though. Oh, stop, please! *(She jumps down)* Just look at all the wildflowers! There must be trillions of them!

> *(She begins to pick them. Lights on her, down on the wagon, as Ethan dons his coat and*

Edward turns to face the audience. Then lights down on Mattie and up on the men, in Winter mode)

EDWARD. It's beautiful up here, isn't it? All that unspoiled whiteness. Frankly I was glad when the opportunity came to get out in the field. A person gets to feeling cooped up after a few months behind a desk, drawing lines and doing figures.

ETHAN. I wouldn't know.

EDWARD. No, I suppose not. *(pauses, then laughs)* I was just thinking what a contrast this is to the landscape I found myself in this time last winter. I was overseeing the contruction of a bridge down in the Florida keys. It seldom gets below freezing down there, you know, and snow is all but unheard of.

ETHAN. Yes, I know. I was down there once. For a good while afterward I could call up the sight of it in winter. Not any more.

EDWARD. So, you've actually been to Florida? Somehow I thought - Well, anyway, it's quite a contrast. *(shivers)* Quite a contrast. *(pause)* How long a ride is it to Corbury Junction, approximately?

ETHAN. No more than an hour and a half. Getting back may take longer.

EDWARD. Oh? Why is that?

ETHAN. Shaping up to storm by evening.

EDWARD *(skeptically)*. You really think so? There's hardly a cloud in the sky. *(no reply)* Well. Would you mind if I had a look through one of your books there, just to pass the time?

ETHAN. I don't mind.

EDWARD *(picks up book from under seat)*. "The Role of Science in Everyday Life." Quite honestly, I'm a bit surprised that you'd be interested in this sort of thing. Do you have a background in the sciences?

ETHAN. Not much of one. I spent a year at the college in Worcester when I was . . . when I was your age.

EDWARD. Really? I hear that's not a bad school. I attended the Institute in Cambridge, myself. Oh, look there. *(Up Center we see two couples "skating" in dim light)* Skaters. What a setting this is - the pond, the trees. This must be a wonderful picnic spot when it's not covered in snow.

ETHAN. It is.

(Lights down on him and Edward. The "skaters" shed their coats and bring forward picnic baskets. The lights come up, warm and summery. Two of the picnickers are Mattie and DENIS EADY, a brash and fashionable fellow. The other two are NED HALE and RUTH VARNUM, an engaged couple about Mattie's age. Ethan, minus the coat and the limp, climbs down from the buckboard and stands watching the picnickers enviously until Mattie spots him.)

MATTIE. Ethan! Come and join us!

ETHAN. I can't. I ain't dressed for it. I was just on my way back from taking a load of lumber, and I thought I'd see if you needed a ride home.

MATTIE. That was thoughtful of you. But I wouldn't like to leave just yet.

ETHAN *(disappointed)*. Oh. Well, that's all right, then. I'll just -

MATTIE. No, no. You mustn't go so soon, either. Sit down and join the fun, please. Here. Have a cup of punch. Go on. It's good. I'll get another one.

NED. Here you are, Mattie.

MATTIE. There, you see? Oh, it's been a wonderful afternoon, hasn't it, fellows?

DENIS. It was.

MATTIE. I wish you'd been able to come. And Zeena, too, of course. We played all sorts of silly games, and went boating on the pond, and - Oh, my!

DENIS. What's wrong, Matt?

MATTIE. I think I've gone and lost my gold locket. It must have come loose when we were playing tag before. Oh . . . tarnation!

RUTH. We'll find it for you, Mattie. Come on, Ned. Let's spread out and search the area.

(They go offstage)

DENIS. It's my fault, for chasing you so hard. Look here, I'll get you another one. My old man has half a dozen lockets at the store.

MATTIE. Thank you, Denis, but this was my mother's. I can't bear to lose it.

ETHAN. I'll help you look.

DENIS. So'll I, of course. We were just over there, in those trees. Maybe it got caught on a branch. *(moves off)*

MATTIE. I really wish you could've been here, Ethan; we had a fine time.

ETHAN. A man has to make a living.

MATTIE. That's so. But there has to be some room in a person's life to do things just for fun, too, doesn't there? Otherwise, it's not living at all, it's just -

ETHAN. Getting by?
MATTIE. Yes. Just getting by. Oh, look! Did you ever see such a beautiful butterfly?
ETHAN. A Great Spangled Fritillary.
MATTIE *(amused)*. What?
ETHAN. That's what it's called - or at least what somebody decided it should be called. A Great Spangled Fritillary.
MATTIE. Where on earth did you learn that?
ETHAN *(pleased with himself)*. College.
MATTIE *(awed)*. You went to College?
ETHAN. For a while. Until my father died. Ah!

(He goes to the spot where the "butterfly" was)

MATTIE. What is it?
ETHAN. Your locket.

(He stoops and retrieves it)

MATTIE. My, you have the sharpest eyes! I'd've walked right by it and never noticed, I know I would. Thank you, Ethan. Would you do up the clasp for me?
ETHAN *(fumbles with it)*. My hands ain't made for this sort of thing.

(He stares at the nape of her neck)

MATTIE. What's the matter? Can't you get it?
ETHAN. No. I can't. *(meaning her, of course. He lets go, backs away)*
MATTIE. Ethan? What's wrong?
ETHAN. I'd better get back, now. I guess you'll have a ride, all right.

MATTIE. Yes, with Denis, but -
ETHAN. I'll see you at home, then.

(He hurries to the wagon. She stares after him, bewildered. Denis enters.)

DENIS. Did you find it, Matt?
MATTIE *(flustered)*. Yes! That is, Ethan did. He found it right off.
DENIS. He's kind of a queer duck, isn't he? Here, let me do that.

(He fastens the locket quickly and deftly)

(Lights down on "picnic" while Mattie and Denis exit. Up on the Fromes' kitchen at Left. ZEENA FROME stands facing the audience, looking through an imaginary window. She is a sallow, unattractive, angular woman of about thirty-five, neat enough but not feminine. Ethan crosses and enters. Zeena glances at him without interest, then back out the window.)

ETHAN. Evening, Zeena.
ZEENA. You see any sign of Mattie on the way?
ETHAN. Wasn't she going to that church picnic?
ZEENA. That don't mean she has to neglect her duties. I've had to start supper myself, never mind that I can hardly bear to put my weight on this one leg of mine.
ETHAN *(washing up at sink)*. Your leg's bothering you now?
ZEENA. It has been, for most of a month.
ETHAN. I don't recall you mentioning it.

ZEENA. More likely you just didn't listen when I did. If I'd 'a' known she'd be there all day and half the night, I'd never have given her the idea to go. I thought it might keep her from complaining about how things here are so different from the way they are in the city.

ETHAN. I never recall her complaining.

(He begins to set the table.)

ZEENA. That's not man's work. Sit down. *(she takes it over)* You know, if you'd've gone to the picnic, you could've brought her back at a decent hour.

ETHAN. I'm not much on social gatherings and the like.

ZEENA. Time was you were more sociable. You used to keep on all the time about how you wanted to move to the city, where there was lectures and libraries, and folks "doing things".

ETHAN. That was a long time ago.

ZEENA. That's so. *(pause)* I don't suppose they bothered to pay you for the lumber.

ETHAN. They'll pay in time. Nobody's got cash money these days.

ZEENA. Least of all us. *(she goes to the window)* Well, looks as if she finally made up her mind to come home. She's got a ride with that Denis Eady. Now there's a family always has some cash money, I guess.

> *(Mattie crosses stage, glances at gravestone, shivers, hurries inside. She looks charmingly flustered, as if Denis might have been sweet-talking her)*

MATTIE. Evening, Ethan. Evening, Zeena. I'm sorry to be so late. We were having such fun, we just let the time get away from us.

ZEENA. Well, things haven't been so much fun here.

MATTIE. You're feeling badly again, ain't you? I'm sorry. I should've been here to fix supper.

ZEENA. I managed. I guess you might as well sit down and have a bite.

MATTIE. Thank you, but I couldn't, not after all we had at the picnic. Do you know, they finished up every crumb of your molasses cake and looked around for more. *(unpacks basket, looks ruefully at the baked beans)* I'm afraid my beans weren't nearly such a success.

ZEENA. Well, if you'd been raised learning more about housework and cooking, and less about playing the piano and trimming hats, you'd've been a sight better off. Of course, if your father had managed his affairs right, he might have left you better provided for.

MATTIE *(looks as if she'd like to protest, but doesn't)*. I guess I'll clear the table and start on the dishes, now. Why don't you just go on up and have yourself a good rest? Maybe you'll feel better.

ZEENA. Not very likely. What've you done with my Mrs. Pinkham's?

MATTIE. Just there, on the sideboard.

ZEENA *(Takes bottle and heads upstairs)*. Be sure you dry that skillet good, else it'll rust again. *(Exits)*

MATTIE. I will. Have a good rest.

(The relief is evident in her face, and in Ethan's. Ethan helps her clear the table.)

MATTIE *(cont)*. No, leave that, Ethan. You've worked hard enough all day.

ETHAN. I don't mind. *(Helps her wash the dishes, enjoying her company)*

MATTIE. I guess you think I should have stood up to her.

ETHAN. She can be hard.

MATTIE. I nearly did. When she spoke about my mama and papa that way, I nearly said something back. My papa worked hard, and my mama was a good woman. She wanted something more for me than just housework and cooking. She wanted me to know about the better things.

ETHAN. She was right to.

MATTIE. Do you think so? I know I ain't anything like as smart as I ought to be. There's lots of things a hired girl could do that come awkward to me still, and I haven't got the strength I should in my arms. But if she'd only tell me, I'd try. If she'd just say, instead of looking at the things I've done with that - that look of hers. I can see she ain't suited with the way I do things, but yet I don't know why, or how to do them better.

ETHAN *(teasing)*. Well, now, she did tell you to be sure and dry the skillet.

MATTIE *(smiles reluctantly)*. That's so. You know, Ethan, if you could tell me sometimes how she wants things done, it'd be a help. You've lived with her longer.

ETHAN. That doesn't mean I know her.

MATTIE. I just don't want her to be always finding fault with me. She might come to decide that I ain't suited, and . . . and I've got no place else to go. Most of my relations, they put money into Papa's business, you see, and when he went under . . . well, they never quite forgave us.

(She's on the verge of crying. Ethan doesn't know how to comfort her.)

ETHAN. It'll be all right.
MATTIE. You think so? *(Ethan nods. She tries to be cheeful, wipes the table)* Thank you. For your help with the dishes, too. I wonder if maybe I shouldn't scrub the floor. It doesn't look bad to me, but I ain't Zeena.
ETHAN. Thank God.
MATTIE. What?
ETHAN. I say, I guess it can wait. You're tired.
MATTIE. You're right about that. It was a fine picnic, though. I wish you could've come. Well, at least you showed up long enough to find my locket. Well. Good night, Ethan.
ETHAN. Good night, Matt.

(After she goes, he pumps water, adds soap, dips in a rag, and starts to scrub. He lights a lamp, goes on scrubbing. Zeena comes down stairs, sees him scrubbing. She coughs, he looks up, startled.)

ETHAN *(cont)*. You're up late.
ZEENA. I couldn't sleep.

(Lights down. Ethan blows out lamp, crosses to wagon, dons coat. Lights up on wagon - winter. Edward turns to audience, looks up at sky.)

EDWARD. You really believe we're in for bad weather?
ETHAN. I don't know much meteorology, but I do know the weather in these parts.

EDWARD. I'm sure you do. That's a desolate looking place, up on the hill. Does anyone live there?

ETHAN. That's my place.

EDWARD. Oh. Well. It looks . . . peaceful. You're certainly off the beaten track here, aren't you?

ETHAN. There was considerable traffic on this road once, before the railroad was carried through to the Flats. After the train began running, nobody every came by here to speak of.

EDWARD. That's the church, down there, I guess?

ETHAN. It used to be. They used to hold dances there, sometimes.

(Dance music. Lights down on the wagon, up on the church area at Down Right. The two picnicking couples are now dancers. Mattie is dancing with Denis. Ethan sheds his coat, approaches, watches. The music stops, the couples move Left. Ethan backs away into the unlighted area. Ned and Ruth call goodnight.)

RUTH. Ain't you riding, Mattie?

MATTIE. Mercy, no; not on such a beautiful night.

(Ruth and Ned exit. Mattie looks around for Ethan.)

DENIS. Your gentleman friend gone back on you? Say, Matt, that's tough. Don't worry, though; I wouldn't be so mean as to tell the other girls. I ain't so lowdown as all that. *(laughs)* But look here, ain't it lucky I got the old man's rig there, just waiting for us?

MATTIE. What on earth do you need your father's rig for, Denis Eady? Your place is no more'n two minutes walk.

DENIS. Why, I just kinder knew I'd want to take a ride tonight. You just wait here and I'll pull her round.

MATTIE. No, don't bother.

DENIS *(tries to take her arm)*. Oh, come on, Matt. You know you want to -

MATTIE *(slips away)*. Good night, Denis! I hope you have a lovely ride!

(Denis shrugs, exits)

ETHAN *(coming downstage)*. Mattie!

MATTIE. Ethan! Where were you?

ETHAN. Think I'd forgotten you?

MATTIE. I thought maybe you couldn't come back for me.

ETHAN. Couldn't? What did you think would stop me?

MATTIE. I knew Zeena wasn't feeling any too good today.

ETHAN. Oh, she's in bed long ago. Did you mean to walk home all alone?

MATTIE. Oh, I ain't afraid.

ETHAN. If you thought I wasn't coming, why didn't you ride home with Denis Eady?

MATTIE. How did you know? Where were you? I never saw you!

ETHAN *(pleased with himself)*. Come on. *(As they cross, they stop at Down Center and look out over the "sledding hill")* In another month or so, this hill'll be covered with people coasting on sleds.

MATTIE. Oh, that sounds like such fun! I never got to do that in the city.

ETHAN. Would you like to come down and coast some night, come winter?

MATTIE. Could we, Ethan? That'd be lovely. It's such a steep hill. It must make for a thrilling ride.

ETHAN. We can come some night when there's a moon. It's best then.

MATTIE. Good. If it was very dark, a person might run smack into that big elm. Ruth Varnum said she and Ned Hale came just as near running into it one time. She was sure they'd be killed. *(shivers)* Wouldn't it have been awful? They're so happy.

ETHAN. Ned ain't much for steering. I guess I could take you down all right.

MATTIE. I know you could. Even so, that elm is dangerous. It ought to be cut down.

ETHAN. Would you be afaid of it with me?

MATTIE *(haughtily).* I told you, I ain't the kind to be afraid. *(They walk on)* There must be a trillion stars out tonight. Are there that many, do you think?

ETHAN. There are more than a person could ever hope to count. We just can't see them all.

MATTIE. You can't see them half so well as this in the city - for all the lights, you know. Do you know the constellations at all?

ETHAN. Some. That's Orion, over yonder. You see those three bright stars in a row? That's his belt. The big fellow to his right, that's Aldebaran. And the bunch of little ones, like bees swarming, that's the Pleiades.

MATTIE. I wish I knew half the things you know about nature and such. The only one I recognize for certain is the Big Dipper. Do you know that song about it - about the Drinking Gourd? *(Ethan shakes his head. She begins singing the song about slavery and escaping to freedom)* "Follow the Drinking Gourd; follow the Drinking Gourd. For the Old Man is a-waiting for to carry you to freedom; follow the Drinking Gourd." *(They near the gravestones, Ethan stops)* Do we have to stop? I don't care much for graveyards. *(No reply. She moves close to him)* What are you thinking, Ethan?

ETHAN. Oh, nothing much.

MATTIE. Yes you were. I could see it in your face.

ETHAN. Well . . . I guess I was just thinking how we look up at those stars and we long to be able to go up there, and in the end the only place we manage to get to is . . . here.

MATTIE. Didn't you ever think of selling the place off, and going someplace else, someplace new?

ETHAN. Of course I did. A hundred times. But nobody wants a worked-out farm and an old mill that barely pays its way, and both of them mortgaged to the hilt. Besides, Zeena would never leave the place. She says she likes a place where she's known . . . even if it is only for being sick, I guess. She won't leave until they day they - She won't leave.

MATTIE. I don't mean to pry, Ethan, but why did you - I mean, how did you and she come to be together? You don't have to answer that.

ETHAN. I don't mind, seeing as it's you. Her family and mine are related, you see, and when my mother took ill, Zeena came over to help do for her. I'm afraid I'm not much use at that sort of thing. But Zeena, she seemed to know just what was wanted. She tended Mother night and day, and cooked meals, and kept the place clean. When the time came, she was the one that thought to send for the undertaker, and to settle who got what from Mother's things. I guess . . . I guess I just couldn't make out how I was going to get along without her. It wasn't too long after that, that I realized the reason why she was so handy tending to other folks' complaints. It was because she'd spent so much tending to her own.

MATTIE. She does seem to make the most of them, sometimes. I'm sorry. That was unkind of me. I ought to try and be more understanding, I know I should.

(They have crossed to the house. Ethan turns Mattie to face him)

ETHAN. You are, Matt. You are understanding. And you're kind, too, and -

(They are within a hair's breadth of embracing, but propriety and duty - and Zeena's proximity - won't let them. Mattie turns away. Ethan scowls and fishes under the doormat for the key.)

ETHAN *(cont)*. The key - it ain't here.
MATTIE. Maybe Zeena forgot to leave it.
ETHAN. Her? She never forgets anything.
MATTIE. Well, maybe it fell off in the grass.

(Ethan takes out a barn-burner match, strikes it, searches. Zeena mimes opening the door. She carries a lamp that throws her features into skeletal relief.)

ETHAN. Guess you forgot about us.
ZEENA. No, I didn't put the key out because I was up. I felt too mean to sleep. *(Takes a dose of medicine)*

MATTIE. I'm sorry, Zeena. Is there anything I can do?

ZEENA. No. You might have finished cleaning up here before you ran off to that dance.

(Mattie tidies up. Zeena starts upstairs)

ETHAN. I guess I won't come up yet a while.

ZEENA. For the land's sake, why not? What would you do down here?

ETHAN. Well, I - I've got the mill accounts to go over.

ZEENA. At this time of night? You'd better get your sleep. You've got a big order to fill tomorrow, don't you?

ETHAN. Not so big. *(Glances furtively at Mattie, who looks away, starts up the stairs ahead of Zeena)* Still, I suppose you're right. *(Lights down)*

(Lights up. Ethan is standing in the kitchen, shaving in the light from the lamp. Zeena comes downstairs.)

ZEENA. The doctor don't want I should be left without anybody to do for me.

ETHAN. Nobody to do for you?

ZEENA. If you say you can't afford a hired girl when Mattie goes.

ETHAN. Why on earth should Mattie go?

ZEENA. Well, when she gets married, I mean.

ETHAN *(cuts himself, puts a dab of paper on it)*. She'd never leave us as long as you need her help.

ZEENA. I wouldn't have it said that I stood in the way of a poor girl like Mattie marrying a smart fellow like Denis Eady. And the doctor don't want I should be left without anybody. He wanted I should speak to you about a girl he's heard about, that might come.

ETHAN *(laughs)*. Denis Eady! If that's all, then I guess there's no hurry to look around for a girl.

ZEENA. All the same, I'd like to talk to you about it.

ETHAN. All right. But I haven't got the time now. *(checks watch)* I'm late getting to the mill as it is.

ZEENA. I guess you're always running late, since you took to shaving every morning.

> *(Ethan is tempted to reply, but thinks better of it. As he's leaving, Mattie comes downstairs. She waves to him, unseen by Zeena. He starts to wave back, then stops himself.)*

ETHAN. See you at dinner, I guess. *(Exits. Lights down)*

> *(Lights up on wagon. Ethan is working beneath it, perhaps tightening a turnbuckle or a bolt. Mattie enters with a lard can containing his lunch. Ethan glances up, and, seeing Mattie's legs, sits up, hitting his head on the wagon bed.)*

MATTIE. Ethan? *(laughs, but is concerned, too)* Oh, Ethan!

ETHAN *(stoically, rubbing his head)*. Hello, Matt.

MATTIE. Are you all right?

ETHAN. I've been better, but I've been worse, too.

MATTIE. I didn't mean to startle you. I just thought I'd save you having to make a trip up to the house for your dinner.

ETHAN. A picnic, eh? That's thoughtful of you.

MATTIE. It's just some sandwiches and tea. Don't worry, I didn't pack any of my famous baked beans. *(awkward silence)* Well. I guess I'd better get on back. Zeena'll be wanting her hot water bottle warmed up.

ETHAN. I'll walk a ways with you. *(they cross Left)* I suppose what folks say is true.

MATTIE. Why, what do folks say?

ETHAN. About you and Denis Eady.

MATTIE. Me and Denis - *(laughs)* Who would say such a thing? Anybody that knows me knows better. Who told you such a thing? *(no reply)* It was Zeena, wasn't it?

ETHAN. She said you'd be leaving us soon.

MATTIE. Leaving you? But I never led her to think - Oh, Ethan, does she mean she ain't suited with me any more?

ETHAN. She didn't say so.

MATTIE. She wouldn't say it, not in so many words. But she'd make it clear.

ETHAN. Maybe not to me. Anyway, I told her you'd stay on as long as you were needed. But I wasn't sure that was how you felt.

MATTIE. You weren't sure? I've never complained, have I? Not really.

ETHAN. Then you don't want to leave us?

MATTIE *(softly, brokenly)*. Where'd I go, if I did?

ETHAN. You ain't - you ain't crying, are you, Matt?

MATTIE. No. Of course I'm not.

ETHAN. Maybe it's selfish to make you stay on here, Matt. Maybe you'd do best to get away now, before you end up staying like them - *(nods at the gravestones)* forever.

MATTIE. Oh, Ethan! You want me to go, too?

ETHAN. *Want* you to go? *(more subdued)* What I want doesn't signify. I was thinking of what's best for you.

MATTIE. I believe I can decide that for myself. *(puts a hand on his arm)* You go on back now. Your tea'll be getting cold. See you at supper.

(He watches until she goes in. Lights down.)

(Lights up on kitchen. Ethan enters. His old valise and a hatbox are sitting at the foot of the stairs. He stares at them in alarm, obviously thinking that Mattie is leaving.)

ETHAN. Mattie? Mattie, why are the - *(He turns to point to the luggage. Zeena comes downstairs with a dress on a hanger. She holds it up to the light, brushes it)* Evening, Zeena.

ZEENA. I guess this don't look completely out of date, does it?

MATTIE. It looks fine, Zeena. You want me to touch it up for you?

ZEENA. I'll do it myself. I don't want it should be scorched.

ETHAN *(joshing her)*. Stepping out, are you?

ZEENA. I've got my shooting pains so bad, I'm going over to Springfield tomorrow to spend the night with Aunt Martha Pierce and see that new doctor she's told me about.

ETHAN. Springfield?

ZEENA. You have some objection to that?

ETHAN. Well, it's just that the last time you went to a doctor in Springfield you came home with that electric battery that cost twenty dollars and you never did make any use of.

ZEENA. I told you, this is a new doctor.

ETHAN. Well, I just hope he knows more about electricity than the old one.

ZEENA. I presume you can drive me over with the sorrel in time to catch the train from Bettsbridge.

ETHAN. Oh. *(glances at Mattie)* Well, let me think, now . . .

ZEENA. Well, if you're going to be too *busy*, maybe you could let Jotham Powell drive me. All I know is, I can't go on the way I am much longer. The pains are clear away down to my ankles, now, or I'd 'a' walked into town and asked Michael Eady to let me ride on his grocery wagon. I'd have had to wait at the station, but I'd sooner have done that than to put you out.

ETHAN. No, no, of course I'll get Jotham to drive you over. I'd take you over myself, only I've got to collect cash for a delivery.

ZEENA. Cash? From who?

ETHAN *(lying)*. Why . . . from Andrew Hale.

ZEENA *(sniffs skeptically)*. I'll believe that when I see it. *(She drains the last of her medicine and hands the empty bottle to Mattie)* That medicine ain't done me a speck of good, but I guess I may as well use it up. If you can get the taste out of the bottle, it'll do for pickles. *(Lights down)*

(Lights up on the livery stable area, where Andrew Hale waits. Ethan climbs down from the wagon.)

HALE. Hello, Ethe! How's things up your way?

ETHAN. I can't complain.

HALE. Well, you could, but I doubt it'd do you much good. How's Zeena?

ETHAN. About the same. *(Starts to say more, is interrupted)*

HALE. That's a shame. I guess Mattie's all right, though, is she?

ETHAN. Oh, yes. She's - she's all right. Say -

HALE. That girl needs to find herself a beau. She waits too long, she's liable to end up the same as - *(clears throat)* Well, she's liable to end up an old maid. You know my Ned and Ruth Varnum have set the date, don't you?

ETHAN. That's good news. Listen, Andrew. I was wondering . . . that is . . . I need to have fifty dollars toward the lumber.

HALE. Fifty dollars! You mean cash? Now?

ETHAN *(embarrassed, but prideful)*. That's right.

HALE. Well, now. You never objected before to giving me three months. You plan on buying yourself a grand piano, or what? Or maybe you mean to put up a new wing on that house of yours. You know, if that's the case, I'll be glad to help you with the construction.

ETHAN. No, no, nothing like that. It's just that I told - Well, it's no matter. If you don't have it, you don't. I'd better get this unloaded and get back before it starts getting dark.

HALE. See here - you ain't in a tight place, are you, Ethe?

ETHAN. No. *(pauses, but his pride won't let him retract)* Not a bit.

HALE. Well, that's good. I don't mind saying I am, a bit. Fact is, I was going to ask you to give me a little extra time on that payment. You see, I'm fixing up a little house for Ned and Ruth. I'm glad to do it, but it costs. The young people like things nice. You know how it is. It's not so long ago since you fixed up your own place, for Zeena.

ETHAN. No so long? It seems as if it was - Well, never mind. I'd best get this unloaded. Got to pick up a few things at Eady's before I go home.

(Denis enters)

DENIS. Good, good. The more business the better. Hello, Ethe.

ETHAN. Denis.

DENIS *(to Hale)*. I'll be taking my old man's rig out for a couple of hours.

HALE. You sure it's all right with him?

DENIS. Sure, I'm sure. A man can't go courting on foot, now, can he?

(Winks at Ethan. He and Hale exit. Ethan pounds the back of the wagon.)

ETHAN. Damnation!

(Ruth and Ned stroll on at Right, whispering and laughing. They stop, Ned takes Ruth in his arms, kisses her. Ruth notices that Ethan is watching, backs away.)

RUTH. Hello, Ethan.

(Embarrassed and envious, Ethan waves awkwardly. Ruth and Ned exit. Lights down.)

(Lights up on kitchen. Ethan crosses, looks around for a sign of Denis Eady's rig, then hurries to the door. He rattles the door handle; it's locked.)

ETHAN. Hello, Matt? Mattie?

(Mattie appears with the lamp, as Zeena did several nights before. But instead of looking skeletal, she looks alluring. Her hair is done up with a ribbon. The table is set with a tablecloth and food, including fresh doughnuts.)

ETHAN *(cont)*. Hello. You look . . . fine.
MATTIE. Don't stand there gawking. Come in.
ETHAN. The table looks fine, too.
MATTIE. Thank you.
ETHAN. Well, Matt; any visitors?
MATTIE. Just one.
ETHAN. Oh. It was Denis Eady, I expect.
MATTIE. Why, no. It was Jotham Powell. He came in after he got back from taking Zeena to the station, and asked for a drop of coffee before he went down home.

ETHAN *(relieved)*. Is that all? Well, I hope you made out to let him have it.

MATTIE. Of course.

ETHAN. I guess he got - he got over to the station all right.

MATTIE. Oh, yes. In plenty of time.

(The thought of Zeena has thrown a pall over things.)

ETHAN. Oh, I nearly forgot. *(Pulls a bag from his pocket)* Here.

MATTIE. Oh, my, Ethan! I haven't had any peanut brittle in ever so long! What we need is a fancy dish to put it in. Zeena has one somewhere. She's showed it to me. *(roots through the cupboard)* Here it is. *(She takes out a red cut-glass dish and empties the candy into it)* There! Well? Ain't you going to sit down?

ETHAN. You bet I am. Oh. Here. *(awkwardly holds chair for her)*

MATTIE. Thank you, sir! *(pours tea for him, hands him a doughnut, which he gratefully accepts as a chance to avoid talking)*

ETHAN. Good.

MATTIE. Thanks.

ETHAN. Looks as if it might decide to snow.

MATTIE. You don't say so? Do you suppose it'll interfere with Zeena - with her getting back? *(realizes how this sounds, she's flustered)*

ETHAN. Never can tell. It drifts pretty bad on the tracks sometimes.

> *(More awkward silence. Mattie reaches to offer him another doughnut, knocks the peanut brittle dish to the floor)*

MATTIE. Here, would you like another - Oh, the dish! Oh, no! *(She kneels to pick up the pieces)* Ethan, it's all to pieces! What'll Zeena say?

ETHAN. Maybe she don't need to know. Look now, you've cut yourself.

> *(He takes her hand, presses his handkerchief to the wound.)*

MATTIE. But she set so much store by it. She never meant it should be used. She'll want to know why I got it out, and what'll I say?

ETHAN. Like I said, she needn't know anything about it. I'll get another one just like it tomorrow.

MATTIE. Oh, you'll never find another one, not here. She told me it was a wedding present, and it came all the way from her aunt in Philadelphia. That's why it meant so much to her. Oh, Ethan! What in the world should I do? *(starts to cry)*

ETHAN. Don't, Mattie, don't. Here, give me the pieces.

MATTIE. Why? What are you going to do?

ETHAN *(hides them far back in the cupboard)*. There. She's not likely to come across it there, at least not until I can find a match for it. Now let's finish our supper.

MATTIE. I'm not so hungry any more. You go ahead.

(Mattie sweeps up the peanut brittle, clears things from the table, takes up a bit of sewing and sits down in Zeena's chair to work on it.)

ETHAN *(looking out "window")*. Most a full moon tonight. Too bad the snow's so late coming. We could have gone coasting.

MATTIE. Oh, there'll be lots of other nights.

ETHAN. You do want to go, though.

MATTIE. Of course.

ETHAN. It'll have to be a night like tonight, when there's plenty of moonlight. That's an ugly corner down by the big elm.

MATTIE. I wouldn't be scared, not even in the dark.

ETHAN. Oh, no! Well, I'd be scared. Anyway, we'll go some night soon. For tonight, I guess we're well enough here.

MATTIE. Yes, we're well enough here.

(Silence. Then Ethan tries to converse in the offhand manner of Denis Eady.)

ETHAN. Oh, say, what do you think I saw under the Varnum spruces on my way home? I saw a friend of yours, getting kissed.

MATTIE *(embarrassed)*. I suppose it was Ruth and Ned.

ETHAN *(nods, embarrassed, too)*. I guess - I guess they've set the date and all.

MATTIE *(wistfully)*. Yes. Ruth says they mean to be married next June. *(she pours him a cup of tea)*

ETHAN. It'll be your turn next, I shouldn't wonder.

MATTIE *(a nervous laugh)*. Why do you keep on saying that?

ETHAN. I guess I do it to get used to the idea.

MATTIE. Zeena hasn't said anything more, has she? About me - about me leaving?

ETHAN. No. Has she to you?

MATTIE. No. I just fancied she's been more . . . more cool towards me lately.

ETHAN. You can't tell, with Zeena.

MATTIE. Maybe I'm making more out of it than I should. Let's not think about it any more, shall we?

ETHAN. No. Let's not. *(pause)* I wish you wouldn't sit there.

MATTIE. Why ever not? It's the place nearest the stove.

ETHAN. All the same. It's Zeena's chair.

MATTIE. You think she'd mind?

ETHAN. Maybe not. But I do. It's as if . . . well, it don't matter.

MATTIE. Yes, it does, if you don't like it. *(changes chairs)* There. Is that better?

ETHAN. Yes.

(Silence. She spreads the fabric out on the table top. He takes hold of the end, as if taking her hand, and then raises it to his lips. There is a banging sound O.S. They look up, startled.)

MATTIE. What was that?

ETHAN. Just the wind, banging the barn door, I guess.

MATTIE. Oh. I thought it might be -

ETHAN. She couldn't be back this soon.

MATTIE. No, I guess not. I just always feel as if . . . as if she's watching me, even when she's not in the room. Waiting for me to do something wrong.

ETHAN. You couldn't do anything wrong, Matt. Not really.

MATTIE *(laughs, embarrassed)*. Tell Zeena that. But I guess you can't, can you?

ETHAN. No.

MATTIE. It's gotten so cold in here. I guess I'll go on up to bed. Good night, Ethan.

ETHAN. Good night, Matt. *(Lights down)*

(Lights up. Mattie is in the kitchen. Ethan comes downstairs.)

ETHAN. Morning, Mattie. No need to fix a breakfast. I've got to take a load of lumber down to Andrew Hale, and I'd better do it early. That way there'll be some time before . . . *(He turns to go)*

MATTIE. Ethan! *(He turns back. She hands him a bottle of tea, wrapped in cloth. Their hands touch briefly.)* Here's some tea to take along. It's cold out.

ETHAN. Thanks. Zeena's never once thought to do something like that. I'll try to be back early.

MATTIE. You won't forget to try and find a dish? I'll find some way of paying for it.

ETHAN. No need for that. *(Lights down)*

(Lights up on livery stable area. Ethan jumps down, Hale enters)

HALE. Hello, Ethe. You better come in for something warm when you're done there.

ETHAN. Thanks, but Matt - I've brought something along. Another time, maybe. I'll unload this soon as I come back from Eady's.

HALE. Eady's again, eh? You must have come into some money.

ETHAN. I don't know where it'd come from. Besides, if I had any to spare, I wouldn't giving it to Eady's. I'd be doing something worthwhile with it.

HALE. Worthwhile, eh? What do you have in mind?

ETHAN. Hard to say. Maybe I'd take a trip. Out West maybe. They say there's lots of opportunity out there.

HALE. Who says that?

ETHAN. Why, the newspaper. See here. Trips to the West. *(pulls the paper out from under the wagon seat)*

HALE. Hell, Ethan, that's just an advertisement. They'll say anything to get your money.

ETHAN. All the same. I hear it's beautiful country.

HALE. Maybe so. But think of it. You wouldn't know a soul out there, and no one'd know you from Adam.

ETHAN. You're right, Andrew. You're right. *(Turns, goes upstage to where Denis Eady sits on a chair, whittling idly)*

DENIS. Why, hello, Ethe. Ain't seen you around much lately. Been sticking pretty close to home, have you?

ETHAN. I've been busy . . . *working*. Your dad around?

DENIS. Oh, he's down the street someplace. Getting his ears lowered, most likely. Anything I can help you with? I don't know the merchandise like the old man does, but if it's something real easy I guess I might manage to locate it for you.

ETHAN *(reluctantly)*. Would you know if he has any cut-glass dishes? Like a pickle dish, I guess.

DENIS *(grimaces)*. A pickle dish, eh? That's a tough one. You have to have it right away, do you?

ETHAN. Yes.

DENIS *(rising lazily)*. Well, let's have a look. Let's see. If I was a pickle dish, where'd I be? This anything like what you're looking for?

ETHAN. No. Too small. And I was wanting red glass.

DENIS. Oh, *red* glass. Well, if you're going to be picky. This ain't Springfield, you know. *(looks some more)* Speaking of Springfield, did Zeena get back from her trip yet?

ETHAN. No. I expect her this evening.

DENIS. Think that doctor in Springfield will do her any good? God knows, she's tried every patent medicine we've ever stocked. You're lucky Mattie's so strong and healthy. Good looking, too.

ETHAN. Do you have a pickle dish, or don't you?

DENIS. Well, now, I guess we don't. Not the particular kind you seem to want, anyway. If you'd care to wait until Dad gets back, maybe he can - *(He turns. Ethan has already gone back to the Livery Stable)* Well. I wonder what's eating him? *(Lights down)*

(Lights up on kitchen. Mattie is at the stove. She looks up, startled, as Ethan bursts in.)

ETHAN. I couldn't find a dish anywhere that's anything like it, Mattie -

MATTIE. Oh, Ethan! Zeena's here!

ETHAN. What? But the sorrel's not in the barn -

MATTIE. Jotham brought some goods back from town, and he took the rig home with him.

ETHAN. How is she?

MATTIE. I don't know. She went right up to her room.

ETHAN. She didn't say anything?

MATTIE. No.

ETHAN. All right, don't fret. It could be weeks before she notices that dish isn't in its place. By that time maybe I'll have a chance to -

(Zeena, still in her traveling clothes, comes downstairs.)

MATTIE. Zeena! Supper's about ready. Come sit down.

ZEENA. I don't feel as if I could touch a morsel.

ETHAN. You're tired after the long ride, I guess.

ZEENA. I'm a good deal sicker than you think.

ETHAN. I - I hope that's not so.

ZEENA. I've got . . . complications. *(Looks meaningfully at Mattie)*

MATTIE. I'll just go and straighten myself up a bit before we eat. *(Exits)*

ETHAN. Complications? Is that what this new doctor told you?

ZEENA. He says any regular doctor would have wanted me to have an operation.

ETHAN. An operation? Nobody ever told you that before. What do you know about this doctor, anyway?

ZEENA. I don't need anybody to tell me I'm losing ground. Everybody can see it - everybody but you. As for Dr. Buck, he's well respected. Eliza Spears says she was wasting away with kidney trouble before she went to him, and now she's up and around and singing in the choir.

ETHAN. Well. I'm glad he's a good one. I guess you'd better do what he says.

ZEENA. I mean to. *(pause)* He says I oughtn't to do a thing around the house. He wants I should have a hired girl.

ETHAN. A hired girl?

ZEENA. Aunt Martha found me one, right off. Everybody said I was lucky to get a girl to come away out here, and I agreed to give her a dollar extry just to make sure. She'll be over tomorrow afternoon, on the train.

ETHAN *(stunned)*. If you meant to take on a girl, you ought to have said so before you started.

ZEENA. How could I? How did I know what Dr. Buck would say?

ETHAN. Oh, Dr. Buck! *(a short, bitter laugh)* Did Dr. Buck say how I was to pay this girl's wages?

ZEENA. No, he didn't! I'd 'a' been ashamed to tell him you grudged me the money to get my health back - and after I lost it nursing your own mother.

ETHAN. My mother! You really believe that.

ZEENA. Everyone knows it's so. All my folks allowed that it was the least you could do to marry me, after all I done.

ETHAN. Oh, God! *(lowers his voice, not wanting Mattie to hear)* Now, look here, Zeena. You know I ain't got the money to hire a girl. You'll just have to send her back.

ZEENA. The doctor says it'll be the death of me if I go on slaving the way I do. He says he doesn't know how I've stood it as long as I have.

ETHAN. *Slaving?* *(pause)* All right. You shan't lift a hand if he says so. I'll do everything around the house myself.

ZEENA. You can't manage to keep up the farm and the mill as it is. Better just to send me to the almshouse and be done with it. I guess there's been Fromes there before this.

ETHAN. I ain't got the money, Zeena, that's all there is to it.

ZEENA. I thought you was to get money from Andrew Hale.

ETHAN. You know Andrew Hale never pays under three months.

ZEENA. Why, you told me yesterday he was going to pay you cash. That was why you couldn't drive me to the train.

ETHAN. That was . . . a misunderstanding.

ZEENA. So you ain't got the money.

ETHAN. No.

ZEENA. And you ain't going to get it.

ETHAN. No.

ZEENA. Well, I couldn't know that when I hired the girl, now, could I?

ETHAN. No. But you know it now. I'm sorry, but it can't be helped. You married a poor man, Zeena. I'll do the best I can for you.

ZEENA *(strangely unperturbed)*. Oh, I guess we'll make out.

ETHAN. Of course we will. There's a whole lot more I can do for you, and Mattie -

ZEENA. There'll be Mattie's board less, anyways.

ETHAN. Mattie's board?

ZEENA *(brittle laugh)*. You didn't suppose I was going to keep *two* girls, did you? No wonder you were scared of the expense.

ETHAN. But - but Mattie's not a hired girl. She's your relation.

ZEENA. She's a pauper that's been nothing but a burden on us. I kept her most of a year. Let somebody else in the family support her a while.

MATTIE *(O.S.)*. Zeena? Should I bring down your medicine?

ZEENA. No, I'm coming up. *(rises)*

ETHAN. You ain't really going to do it, Zeena?

ZEENA. Do what?

ETHAN. Send Mattie away.

ZEENA. I never bargained to take her on for life!

ETHAN. You can't put her out of the house like a - like a thief, a poor girl without friends or money. She's done her best for you, and she's got no place else to go.

She's your kin. If you send her away, what'll folks think of you? What'll they say?

ZEENA. I know well enough what they say about my having kept her as long as I have.

ETHAN *(taken aback by this semi-accusation)*. You ought to at least let her stay on a while yet, at least until she finds another position someplace.

ZEENA. The new girl will be over tomorrow, and she's got to have someplace to sleep.

(Angry, Ethan goes to the window. Zeena passes Mattie on the way upstairs)

MATTIE. I hope Zeena isn't worse.
ETHAN. No.
MATTIE. You'd better sit down. You must be starving. *(Ethan sits and fills his plate, begins to eat mechanically, but it seems to stick in his throat. He lays down his fork)* What's wrong Ethan? Don't it taste right?

ETHAN. Yes, it's first rate. I just -

(Unable to sit still, he rises and goes to the door)

MATTIE. Ethan, there's something wrong. I knew there was! Tell me.

ETHAN. Oh, Matt, I -

(Impulsively he pulls her to him)

MATTIE. What is it? What's wrong?
ETHAN. You can't go, Matt! I'll never let you!
MATTIE *(steps back, bewildered)*. Go? Must I go? *(Ethan can't meet her gaze)* Ethan, what's happened? Is Zeena mad with me?

ETHAN. No, no, it ain't that. This new doctor's got her scared. You know she believes all they say the first time she sees them, and this one's told her that she won't get well unless she lays up and don't do a thing around the house, not for months.

MATTIE. And she wants somebody handier than me. Is that it?

ETHAN. That's what she says tonight.

MATTIE. If she says it tonight, she'll say it tomorrow. I know Zeena well enough to know that.

ETHAN. It ain't fair. I've given up everything else I care about because of her, and now . . . Oh, Matt, where'll you go?

MATTIE. I don't quite know. I guess I could find something like I had before, at the department store.

ETHAN. But you hated that, you said.

MATTIE. And you once said a person does what's wanted.

ETHAN. You deserve better than that. You deserve a home and - You can't go, Mattie. I won't let you. She's always had her way; now I mean to have mine.

(He sees the warning look on Mattie's face. Zeena has come downstairs again.)

ZEENA. I feel a mite better, and Dr. Buck says I ought to eat all I can to keep up my strength, even if I ain't got the appetite for it. *(She sits and serves herself.)* Ain't you going to eat?

(Mattie sits obediently, but Ethan turns away, as if determined to resist her in some small way.)

ETHAN. I've got no appetite either. I'm going out to check on the animals. *(Outside, he looks up at the sky.)* All the stars are hiding. It's gonna snow, all right. *(Lights down.)*

(Lights up on the wagon. Ethan wears his coat and his twisted manner. Edward sits beside him)

EDWARD. You think it'll snow before evening, then?

ETHAN. I'd be surprised if it doesn't. There's your power house.

EDWARD. I'm grateful to you for the ride. Can I count on you for this evening?

ETHAN *(nods)*. Better not be too late, or we'll catch it.

EDWARD. Will five o'clock be all right? That should give me enough time.

(Ethan nods again, clucks to his "team". Lights down)

(Lights up on house. Zeena sits in her rocker, rubbing uncomfortably at her belly.)

ZEENA. That pie of yours always sets a mite heavy, Mattie. I've a mind to hunt up those stomach powders I got last year in Springfield. I ain't tried them in a while. Could be they'll help with the heartburn.

MATTIE. Can I get them for you?

ZEENA. No, I ain't just sure myself where I put them.

(She goes to the cupboard, begins to root around. Alarmed, Mattie backs away. Ethan enters, she signals to him helplessly)

ETHAN. Why don't you sit down, Zeena. I'll find whatever it is -

ZEENA *(she's found the broken dish, and lifts it out, her face white with anger)*. I want to know who done this.

(Mattie starts to own up, Ethan interrupts.)

ETHAN. I done it, Zeena. It was my fault. I bought some peanut brittle, and I thought it needed a decent dish.

ZEENA. Peanut brittle? Why would you buy peanut brittle?

ETHAN. Because I like it.

ZEENA. You never bought it before!

ETHAN. You said the nuts upset your stomach.

MATTIE. No, Ethan. You don't need to shelter me. It was my fault, Zeena. I was the one got it out, and I'm to blame for breaking it.

ZEENA. *You* got it out? What for?

MATTIE. I wanted - I wanted to make the supper table pretty.

ZEENA. You wanted to make the supper table pretty. So you waited till I was gone, and took the one thing I set the most store by and wouldn't ever use, not even when the minister came to dinner. You're a bad girl, Mattie Silver, I've always known it. I was warned of it when I took you in, and I did it anyway, and now you've took from me the one thing I cared for most of all - *(She sobs and vainly tries to put the pieces together. Ethan is stunned. She's taking from him the one thing he cares for, yet she's the one*

46

grieving.) If I'd listened to folks you'd have gone long ago, and this never would have happened.

ETHAN. Don't listen to her, Matt.

MATTIE. No, she's right. I never should have taken it out. I should never have come here to begin with.

ETHAN. Don't say that.

MATTIE. It's true. It would've been better for all of us. *(Runs upstairs)*

> *(Unable to comfort her or confront Zeena, Ethan storms out. He crosses to the wagon, looking up at the sky again)*

ETHAN. Snow. We'll have a foot by morning.

(He mimes going inside the mill. He reaches under the seat for an old horse blanket, pulls out a copy of the Bettsbridge Eagle as well, looks at the advertisement.)

ETHAN *(cont).* Trips to the West. The Land of Opportunity. *(pronounces them reverently)* Wyoming. Montana. California.

> *(He thinks a moment, then takes out an order book and a pencil from under the seat, and writes on the back of a sheet.)*

ETHAN. "Zeena. I've done all I could for you, and I don't see as it's been any use. I don't blame you, nor I don't blame myself. Maybe both of us will do better apart. I'm going to try my luck in the West. You can sell the farm and the mill and keep the money - " *(pauses, laughs bitterly)* Money? What money? Who would ever want to buy this - this graveyard? *(Yanks out the page, crumples it, tosses the order book under the seat, lies down on the seat and covers himself with the horse blanket. Lights down)*

> *(Lights up. Ethan is sleeping under the blanket. Mattie crosses to him, touches him, he wakes.)*

MATTIE. Oh, Ethan. Were you out here in the mill all night? You must be frozen.

ETHAN. How did you know I was here?

MATTIE. I saw you go down the hill and I listened all night, but you didn't come in again.

ETHAN. I might have left. I might have caught a train out West. *(shows her the paper)* But I didn't. I just couldn't bear to be in the house with her.

MATTIE. I know. I don't see how you've stood it as long as you have. *(reads paper)* Don't the names sound appealing, though? Wyoming. Montana. Like some mythical countries.

ETHAN. They might just as well be, as much as it costs to get there. Still, if I were to collect the money Andrew Hale owes for the lumber, it'd just about pay for two fares.

MATTIE. Two?

ETHAN. The trouble is, getting it. If I told him I had to have it for some reason. I could say I needed it to pay for Zeena to have an operation.

MATTIE. That's not so, is it?

ETHAN. No.

MATTIE. You ain't the sort to lie, Ethan.

ETHAN. I ain't the sort to do a lot of things. But maybe it's time I started. What good has being truthful and dutiful ever done me? I'll just go and demand the money, that's all. It's owed to me, and I've a right to collect it.

MATTIE. Well, right now you've got to come up to the house and get warm. I've built a fire and put coffee on.

(They start toward the house)

ETHAN. Careful, it's slippery. Has she said anything to you this morning?
MATTIE. No. I ain't seen her yet.
ETHAN. If she does, don't you take any notice. I guess things'll straighten out. I don't want you should trouble.
MATTIE *(trustingly)*. No, Ethan, I ain't going to trouble.

(They enter, stomping snow from their feet. Zeena is up.)

ZEENA. The new girl will be at the station at five. Jotham will take you over then, so's you can catch the six o'clock for Stamford. I'd like to go over things with you first. I know there's a huckabuck towel missing, and I can't make out what you did with that match safe, the one used to stand behind the stuffed owl in the parlor.
MATTIE. All right.
ETHAN. I'm going down to town for a while. I may not be back for dinner.

(Mattie looks forlorn. He leaves without meeting her gaze. As he passes the headstones, he pauses to stare at them. He walks on, past the sledding hill, to the place where the church was, gazes at it. We hear dance music faintly in the background.

Ethan goes on to the livery stable area. MRS. HALE, a portly woman in her forties, enters.)

MRS. HALE. Why, hello, Ethan. Got another load of lumber for us, have you?

ETHAN. Not today. I need to talk to Andrew, is all.

MRS. HALE. Well, you'll have to go down to the house to do it, I'm afraid. He's laid up with a bad back, and I'm filling in for him as best I can.

ETHAN. I'm sorry to hear that. About his back, I mean.

MRS. HALE. Yes, he twisted it bad yesterday, shoeing a horse. I just wish there was some way I could do the shoeing for him. I don't mind saying, we could use the money, what with the young ones' house and all. *(laughs)* Can't you just see me trying to hold a horse's hoof in my lap? *(pats her ample girth)* Truth to tell, it feels peculiar, just trying to run the stable. This is a man's business. A woman's business is to run things around the house. But a body does what's required sometimes, don't they? I'm sure Mr. Hale will be awake if you want to go down.

ETHAN. No, that's all right. I wouldn't want to bother him. I was just hoping to - Well, it wasn't anything important.

MRS. HALE. If you're sure. I hope that new doctor over to Springfield was able to do some good for Zeena. I don't know anybody around here as has had more illness than her. I always tell Mr. Hale I don't know what she'd 'a' done if she hadn't had you to look after her. I used to say the same about your poor mother, God rest her soul. You're a good man, Ethan, to stand by them like you done.

(Ethan doesn't trust himself to answer, merely nods. Lights down.)

(Lights up on the house. Zeena is outside, wrapped in a quilt, watching for Jotham - or Ethan.)

ETHAN. Where's Mattie?
ZEENA. Inside, getting her trunk.
ETHAN. By herself?
ZEENA. Well, you don't expect me to help -

(Ethan barges inside. Mattie is trying to drag her trunk down the stairs, crying. She lights up when she sees him.)

MATTIE. Ethan! I thought I wasn't ever going to see you again!

ETHAN. Not see me? What do you mean?

MATTIE. You said you mightn't be back for dinner, and then this morning you said about catching a train, and I thought -

ETHAN. You thought I meant to cut it?

(Mattie nods, buries her face in his shoulder.)

MATTIE. I'd better hurry. Jotham will be here any time.

ETHAN. You let go of that. I can do that much, at least. *(He hoists the trunk, heads for the door, then stops)* I'm going to drive you over to the station, Matt.

MATTIE. I think Zeena wants I should go with Jotham.

ETHAN. Never mind what Zeena wants. *(Zeena enters)* When Jotham gets here, tell him I'm driving Mattie over myself.

ZEENA. I want you should stay here this afternoon, Ethan. Jotham can drive Mattie over.

ETHAN. I'm going to drive her over myself.

ZEENA. I wanted you should fix up that stove in Mattie's room before the new girl comes. It ain't been drawing right.

ETHAN. If it was good enough for Mattie, I guess it's good enough for a hired girl.

ZEENA. The new girl told me she's used to a house where they had a furnace.

ETHAN. Then she'd have done better to stay there. Come on, Matt.

MATTIE. Goodbye, Cousin Zeena. I hope the new girl works out. Thank for for having me as long as you have. I'm sorry about the dish.

(No reply. They cross to the wagon, Ethan loads the trunk, they climb on.)

ETHAN. Go 'long. *(pause)* It's early yet. We've got lots of time for a good long ride.

MATTIE. All right. You know where I'd most like to go?

ETHAN. Now, you mean?

MATTIE *(nods)*. I'd like to go around by Shadow Pond, where they had the church picnic last summer.

ETHAN. It won't look like much this time of year. It'll be covered in snow.

MATTIE. Just the same, I'd like to see it again, before I - I just want to see it again. We had such a good time there. Why did you leave so sudden, that day?

ETHAN. I guess I just felt . . . out of place. I'm not like those other fellows.

MATTIE. Thank heavens for that. I was afraid I'd said or done something that made you mad with me.

ETHAN. There's nothing you could say or do that would make me want to leave you. *(pause)* If we could go anyplace at all right now, where would you go?

MATTIE. That's a funny question. If I could go anyplace? I guess if I could go anyplace at all, I'd want to go up there, on the moon. It looks so peaceful up there.

ETHAN. It does, doesn't it? But scientists say it's just a dead piece of rock.

MATTIE. I don't know, then. I don't know where I'd go. Not to Stamford, I know that.

ETHAN *(after a silence)*. What'll you do with yourself, Matt?

MATTIE. I guess I'll get a place in a store all right. I'm a lot stronger now than I was before I came.

ETHAN. Isn't there any of your mother's folks could help you out?

MATTIE. There's none of them I'd ask.

ETHAN. You know there's nothing I wouldn't do for you, if I could. If there was any way . . . any way I could have found to go with you, I would have. I meant to, I truly did. I even started a letter to Zeena, telling her I'd gone West. I thought I'd ask you to go with me. But I couldn't make out any way to raise the money, or to provide for Zeena - I tried for years to sell the farm and the mill, and that's no good. I even went to Andrew Hale, to ask him for the money.

MATTIE. Oh, Ethan. That must have been hard for you.

ETHAN. He didn't have it, no more than I do. Matt - If I could have found a way, would you have?

MATTIE. What's the use, now?

ETHAN. I've got to know. Would you?

MATTIE *(after a pause)*. I used to think about that very thing sometimes, summer nights when the moon was so bright I couldn't sleep.

ETHAN. As long ago as that?

MATTIE. Longer. *(pause)* You must promise to write to me sometimes, Ethan.

ETHAN. What good is that? I want to be able to put out my hand and touch you. I want to care for you, and be there when you're sick and lonesome.

MATTIE. You mustn't trouble about me. I'll manage all right . . . somehow.

ETHAN. How will you, all on your own? But then I suppose you'll find someone soon enough, and marry him.

MATTIE. Oh, Ethan. Don't.

ETHAN. I can't help it, Matt. I'd almost rather have you dead than that.

MATTIE. Oh, I wish I was! I wish I was!

ETHAN. I didn't mean it. Don't let's talk that way.

MATTIE. Why shouldn't we, when it's so? I've been wishing it every minute of the day.

ETHAN. You be quiet, now.

MATTIE. I don't want to be alone, and there's never been anybody good to me but you.

ETHAN. Don't say that, either, when I can't lift a hand to help you.

MATTIE. It's true, all the same. You would if you could, I know that. Oh, look, Ethan. The sledding hill. There's a few folks been using it already.

ETHAN. They've all headed home. It'll be too dark to see, soon.

MATTIE. We never did go down together, like you promised we would.

ETHAN. How'd you like me to take you down now?

MATTIE *(laughs nervously)*. Oh, there isn't time.

ETHAN. There's all the time we want. Look, somebody's left their sled behind. They won't mind if we use it once. Come on.

MATTIE. But the girl - the girl'll be waiting at the station.

ETHAN. Let her wait. You'd have to, if she didn't. Now come on. *(He helps her down, goes to the edge of the stage, lifts up a sled. With a desperate sort of glee, they sit on the sled at the edge of the stage, Mattie in front, Ethan behind.)* All set.

MATTIE. Are you sure you can see well enough?

ETHAN. I could go down with my eyes blindfolded. *(He shoves off. The lights dim and fluctuate to give the impression of speed. Sound of rushing wind, getting louder. They tilt back and forth on the sled. Mattie screams breathlessly)* Don't be scared, Matt!

MATTIE. Watch the elm, watch the elm! *(covers her eyes)*

ETHAN. I'm watching! *(They tumble off the sled, laughing and gasping, pick up the sled and walk upstage a little)* Were you scared I'd run us into it?

MATTIE. I told you, I was never scared with you.

ETHAN. It is a tricky place, though. The least swerve, and we'd never have come up again. But I can measure distance to a hair's breadth - always could.

MATTIE. I always said you had the sharpest eyes. *(looks down the "hill")* I'm glad Ruth and Ned didn't hit the elm that day. The look so happy every time I see them. I'm happy for them.

ETHAN. What about you? You've got a right to be happy, too. *(Turns her to face him)* What'll we do, Matt? What'll we do? *(Kisses her)*

MATTIE. Oh, Ethan, I don't want to go! *(She clings to him. The clock in town chimes five. She pulls away)* I guess it's time. If I miss my train, I'll have no place to go at all. *(They head toward the wagon, then, impulsively)* Ethan. I want you to take me down again.

ETHAN. Down where?

MATTIE. The hill. So we'll never come up any more.

ETHAN. What do you - what do you mean?

MATTIE. Right into the big elm. You said you could. So we'd never have to leave each other any more.

ETHAN. Oh, Matt! You're talking crazy!

MATTIE. I'll be crazy if I have to leave you. I don't know how I'd get along on my own. You said so yourself. And then there'll be that strange girl in the house, and she'll sleep in my bed, where I used to lay nights and listen to hear you come up the stairs. And what about you, Ethan? If you go back there, you might as well be going back to a coffin. You'll suffocate there, with Zeena hanging around your neck like a dead weight. Please. Let's go down one more time, Ethan. Just once, and that'll be the end of it. *(He lets her lead him to the apron. They sit on the sled)* Oh, look. It's clearing up. And just look how bright the first stars are!

ETHAN *(springs to his feet)*. Get up!

MATTIE. No! This is what I want!

ETHAN. I ain't cutting out, Mattie. I just want to sit in front.

MATTIE. Why?

ETHAN. Because. Because I - I want to feel you holding on to me.

MATTIE. But you won't be able to steer from up there, Ethan. And besides, if one of us should. . . . should come away, I don't want it to be me.
ETHAN. Are you sure?
MATTIE. I'm sure.

(They push off. Lights fluctuate, sound of wind comes up, building louder and louder)

ETHAN. We can fetch it; I know we can.
MATTIE. I'm not afraid. Not with you.

(But she closes her eyes, and buries her face against his leg. He looks grimly straight ahead, tilting to steer the sled. Blackout. The sound stops abruptly at the same time. After a moment, the lights come up just enough to reveal Ethan and Mattie sprawled next to the sled. Ethan painfully reaches out to touch Mattie.)

ETHAN *(In a hoarse whisper)*. Oh, Matt . . . I thought we'd fetch it. Matt? Mattie? *(Lights down)*

(Lights up on the buckboard. Ethan is wearing the coat and the twisted manner. Edward approaches and climbs on.)

EDWARD. I was afraid you might not make it.
ETHAN. I said I'd be here.
EDWARD. You said we were in for bad weather, too, and it looks as if you were right.
ETHAN. Don't expect we'll make it all the way back to Starkfield. Better figure on putting up at my place.

EDWARD. Your place? *(unenthusiastically)* Well, if you think that's best.

ETHAN. I don't know that it's best. But sometimes we have to do just what's necessary.

(Lights down, up again)

EDWARD. It's certainly turning cold quickly. Why are we stopping? Mr. Frome? There's nothing here. *(He sees that Ethan is staring at the headstones Stage Left)* Oh. I suppose that's where your family is buried.

ETHAN. Them . . . and a few others.

EDWARD. It must be very few. It's such a small space.

ETHAN. Big enough, I guess. There aren't many Fromes left. *(Starts up the horses)*

> *(Lights up very low on the kitchen. Two figures are dressed in bulky clothing, unrecognizable at first. The figure sitting in a rocking chair is draped with a quilt, hunched over)*

FIRST FIGURE *(in a hoarse voice that we assume must be Zeena's)*. That sounds like him coming in now. I don't know why in the world he has to be out on a night like this, and leave us barely enough wood to keep warm with.

SECOND FIGURE You'll eat some supper tonight, won't you? You can't keep up your strength without you have something hot to eat now and again.

FIRST FIGURE. I don't know if I can. It hurts me so to set up to the table. Maybe if you was to just give me a plate with a little something on it . . .

(Ethan and Edward enter)

ETHAN. My, it's cold in here. The fire must be almost out.

(He turns up the lantern, the lights come up enough so we can see that the woman serving supper is Zeena. The figure in the quilt is still unrecognizable)

FIRST FIGURE *(whining)*. It's only just been made up this very minute. Zeena fell asleep and slept ever so long. I thought I'd be frozen stiff before I could get her to wake up and tend to it.
ETHAN. I'll see to it. This is my wife, Mrs. Frome. *(Edward bows slightly, Zeena nods to him)* And this is . . . this is Miss Mattie Silver.

(The First Figure removes the quilt and we see that it is indeed Mattie, but a pitiful, broken Mattie. She holds out one crippled hand.)

MATTIE. How do you do.

(Edward takes her hand, stares at her. Lights down.)

(Lights up on livery stable area, with Hale and Edward)

HALE. Well, I see you survived the big storm.
EDWARD. Yes. Mr. Frome put me up at his house for the night.
HALE. You don't say? I don't believe but what you're the first stranger who's set foot in that house in ten years. He's that proud, he don't even let his oldest friends

go there. Neither Zeena nor Mattie goes out any more, either. How did they seem?

EDWARD. Mrs. Frome seemed better than I expected. She was very solicitous toward Miss Silver, and surprisingly patient with her.

HALE. That's Zeena for you. She always was able to put aside her own complaints when she had someone around that was worse off. Not that she's ever given up doctoring herself, but she's had the strength to care for those two, and before the accident she thought she couldn't even care for herself.

EDWARD. What sort of accident was it?

HALE. Why, Mattie was in the same smash-up that done that to Ethan. They carried her to our place afterward, since it was closest. Folks could never rightly tell what she and Ethan were doing coasting on that hill when they ought to have been catching a train. Nobody ever knew what Zeena thought, but as soon as the doctor said Mattie could be moved, Zeena took her back to the farm.

EDWARD. And she's been there ever since?

HALE. There was nowhere else for her to go. There was a time, right after the accident, when they all thought Mattie could never live. Well, I say it's a pity she did. If she'd died, then Ethan might have lived. The way they are now, I don't see there's much difference between the Fromes up at the farm and the Fromes down in the graveyard.

(Sound of a train whistle)

HALE *(cont)*. That'll be your train. Where do you go from here?

EDWARD. Out to Montana, to oversee a new power plant.

HALE. Out West, eh?

(Ethan has moved to Center Stage, where Mattie stood upon her arrival. He stands staring at the train longingly as it whistles again.)

(Lights Down.)

* * *

MUSIC USE NOTE

Licensees are solely responsible for obtaining formal written permission from copyright owners to use copyrighted music in the performance of this play and are strongly cautioned to do so. If no such permission is obtained by the licensee, then the licensee must use only original music that the licensee owns and controls. Licensees are solely responsible and liable for all music clearances and shall indemnify the copyright owners of the play(s) and their licensing agent, Samuel French, against any costs, expenses, losses and liabilities arising from the use of music by licensees. Please contact the appropriate music licensing authority in your territory for the rights to any incidental music.

IMPORTANT BILLING AND CREDIT REQUIREMENTS

If you have obtained performance rights to this title, please refer to your licensing agreement for important billing and credit requirements.

www.ingramcontent.com/pod-product-compliance
Lightning Source LLC
Chambersburg PA
CBHW052030290426
44112CB00014B/2452